THE LIFE TALE

LAKSHMI @11

ANJALI

THERE ARE MO WRONGDOINGS AND RIGHTDOINGS THERES A

FIELD OUT THERE FOR JUDJEMENTS

Contents

Foreword

foreward to all authors

Preface

the life is a fairy tale we should live the it should be lived
always be conscious to our actions and spread happiness

Acknowledgements

POETRY IS THE ONLY WAYOUT TO EXPRESS OUR VOICE AND CAN IMPROVE ONESELF TO EXPRESS

Acknowledgements

THE LIFE TALE

CHAPTER ONE

TRAVEL

Enter Caption

"The more you travel and you will more understand the life the journey is you get on you must walk the path leaving all things behind"

you are the solo traveller of you finally you must reach yourselF

Life feels magical to me when i make these associations between past and present..to see how aligned everything is .

Each moment of every day

I will look to Him for His guidance

Each step of the pilgrim way

The pathway that lies before me

Nature, Beauty, Love, God - are our SAFETY NETS for balancing our emotional state..

...holding our mind steady through the RISE AND FALL OF WAVES happening inside us all the time.

CHAPTER TWO

THE VIBE

FREE

There was a time i took pains to explain myself, clarify, seek to understand others.

I am so done with that.

I realised that my energy is precious and my self expression , the way it comes naturally to me, is important for me.

Our bodies are fragile like the ceramic vase.

They are meant to support journey of our soul, the expansion of our consciousness..an inner understanding of the rules of the universe

This One seems to be solving every problem in my mind.

It is there and not there.

It is alive and dead.

It is outside and inside.

It is falling and stationary.

It is wet and dry.

CHAPTER THREE

MOTIVE

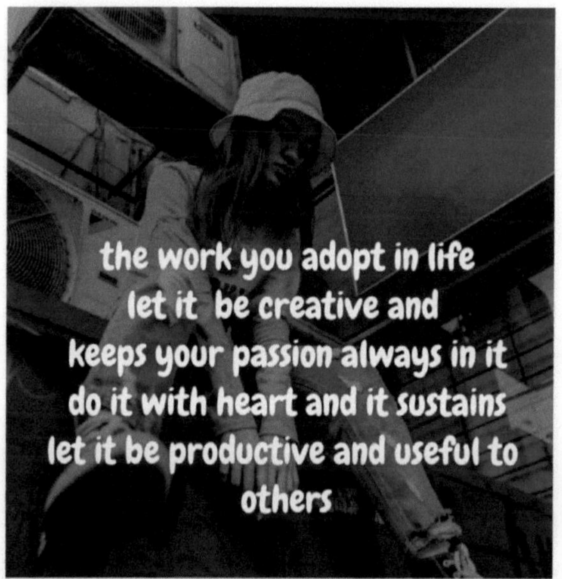

Enter Caption

The world you can perceive is a very small world indeed.

And it is entirely private.

the essence of reality, the perfection of the ultimate truth, the primordially pure ground of being.?

The sky unaffected by any cloud, yet never separate, always embracing.?

Thinking right

is to cognise being the thinker.

All your negative thoughts are not your thoughts.

It is of the world from where you are gathering information and pondering upon it.

That is all about negative thoughts.

Simple.

Now be the thinker and think only when you want to think.

Let's experience.

Connect with Pure Love and Conduct with Pure Wisdom..........

This way you will bravely become complete. The Eternal Flame which is lying dormant within most of us will awaken and it will begin to remain ablaze all the time at the altar of our Being.

With understanding, feeling, and flowing in That wave length, let's all individually and collectively

dance within; pure and clean, calm and serene.........realizing....You will notice that you are attending the birth of something new. Thoughts have dissolved into peace and you have become ONE who embraces all.

If we can be as a small torch on a dark path for others atleast we show the where the next step is.

Without force or demands.

Just a little light to help them see the path and make a choice.

That is really loving and caring guidance without demands.

It is just as simple as that!

We can't just sit down and waith for an amazing future just coming up like that.

It is not a new job partner money or other earthly things.

It is about do our inner work raise and evolve.

Because our new bright future comes from within us.
Not from the earthly world.

CHAPTER FOUR

Thoughts

Enter Caption

I slip into full awareness of all related fields and subjects.

In admitting a new body of evidence, we instinctively

seek to disturb as little a possible, our preexisting

set of ideas and prejudices. your thoughts should be pure like water

The Tidal waves of the Sea leave beautiful marks on the sand of the Shore right after of High Tide and the next tide waves erases the older marks and make new marks to give a message of continuous change to bring happiness and beauty.

Slow down and observe all that is occurring along your path. Do so in order to recognize who has shown up upon your path recently, who has left peacefully every bit as much as those who continue to call you or drop by unannounced suspiciously after you have risen up in vibration. When your energies are ripe for them to pilfer and drain.

Take the time to honor and respect YOUR "SELF" enough to meditate and ask to be shown who is attaching the heavy anchors of THEIR FEARS. Ask to be shown those that are having you drag THEIR ANCHORS.

Their extremely heavy, low vibrational "anchors" they refuse to lift up from the very depths of the very same abyss of despair, shame, low self-esteem, self sabotage, and so on.

FEEL EVERYTHING THAT COMES ACROSS YOUR PATH!

BE THEY GOOD, BAD, OR INDIFFERENT!

ALLOW THESE FEELINGS TO TEACH YOU THAT WHICH MUST BE LET GO OF!

ALLOW THESE FEELINGS TO TEACH YOU THAT WHICH TO EMBRACE!

ALLOW THESE FEELINGS TO TEACH YOU THAT WHICH TO LOOK FORWARD TO!

THIS GOES FOR PEOPLE, PLACES, AND THINGS!

SLOW DOWN!

CHAPTER FIVE

Heaven

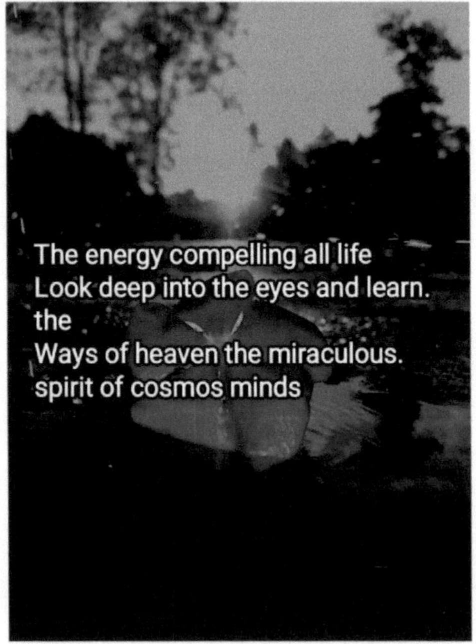

MARK

Mind is a heaven

your breath uprooted the trees and swept away the oceans

Leaving your mark upon this world From the second that you are born

Incredibly fascinating Generations growing, adorn

CHAPTER SIX

KNOW

KNOW THYSELF

"But you don't have to renounce everything. Live in the world the way the tortoise does. The tortoise roams about in the water but keeps its eggs on land.

Its whole mind is on the eggs.

Everything that is perceived in human consciousness is seen as the manifestation

Even in the midst of the crowds of other human beings, viewed from the seat of Pure Consciousness, he recognizes but the One Self that revels every-where. The majestic aloneness felt by a wanderer in a forest is the example Janaka is forced to employ here. Even in a crowd, at some busy market-place, he feels undisturbed as though he is in a deep forest, all alone."

but how can this be? how can the Self need the experience of millennia of suffering due to the ignorance of duality?

it seems to me that there is much more knowing of ignorance than knowing of truth, in fact it is said that the truth cannot be "known" (with the mind).

Stand strong with your bare feet on the ground and with everything that comes from it. Be smarter every day by listening to your intuition, looking at the world with your forehead. Jump, dance, sing, so that you live happier. Heal yourself, with beautiful love, and always remember... you are the medicine

CHAPTER SEVEN

A DAY

When we make peace with outer world..with right knowledge, wisdom, inner awareness..

Our Inner and outer worlds will be in harmony.

Inner world then starts influencing outer world. This is manifesting our true reality.

Survival is a constant fight or flight response.

Thriving is a peaceful place that is rooted in stillness.

You cant run from the shadow but you can invite it to dance.

The dance is rhythm, flow, which comes from being in alignment, heart, mind, body, soul..

May our bodies and minds be healthy. May our thoughts be filled with love.

May our practice be free of obstacles.

Boundaries are vital for all relationships to work and be happy and harmonious!

If you cross others boundaries...what is that telling g them about you? Why would they want to stay in connection with you?

How do you honor your own boundaries?

I got stronger I boundaries when I started going to cuddle events. They are all about boundaries! I loved the.."you are a hell yes, otherwise you are a no". There are no maybes in cuddles...if you "dont know" you are a no!

Life can be that simple too!

CHAPTER EIGHT

Structure

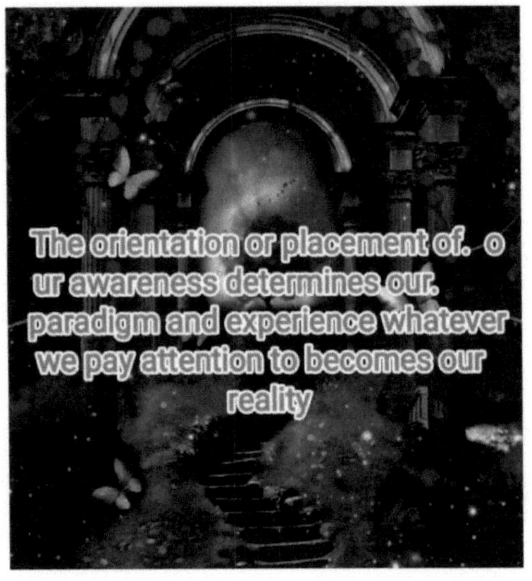

Most of us spend years trying to figure out who we are, wearing multiple masks (or identities), and experiencing incredible highs and lows as a result of these constantly changing identities.

Because in truth, our Essence never changes, even though our identities do. If our essence is water, it does not matter if you pour that water into a cup, a glass, a pitcher, a pot, or anything else. The outer layers will always change, but the inner one never does.

The key to catch is as soon as you realise a thought. switching it to something you appreciate keep peace in your soul

We cannot have others tell us or define us. People around are mirrors.

Some mirrors are clear .they reflect our beauty as is without distortions..

some MIRRORS are not clear..so we see only Whatever we give our attention to, it seems to multiply

Hence one needs to be mindful about what one values.

It can be things we keep in our space, relationships, what we care about, what we are giving our attention and energy to. We either spread ourselves too thin, or we got locked in mental prison, caged by our own beliefs.

CHAPTER NINE

SELF LOVE

This is about transitioning to mindful intentional authentic living ... celebrating self and our relationship with life, the Cosmos.

When our heart becomes transparent...there are no boundaries and limitations. We are just being OURSELVES. Whatever comes to us, uplifts us..teaches us how to rise and shine in many ways.

Each person shines different light on us..make us connect with "new self" "new shade" within.

This thing called consciousness..is shaping or coloring our energy (emotional field) ..which gets translated to intentions, thoughts, feelings ..and we also have the ability to shape our consciousness...using our Free-Will.

We do that through intentional mindful living...by setting intentions..by choosing who we wish to be.. by being led and guided by HIGHER uplifting VISION.

CHAPTER TEN

LIFE STYLE

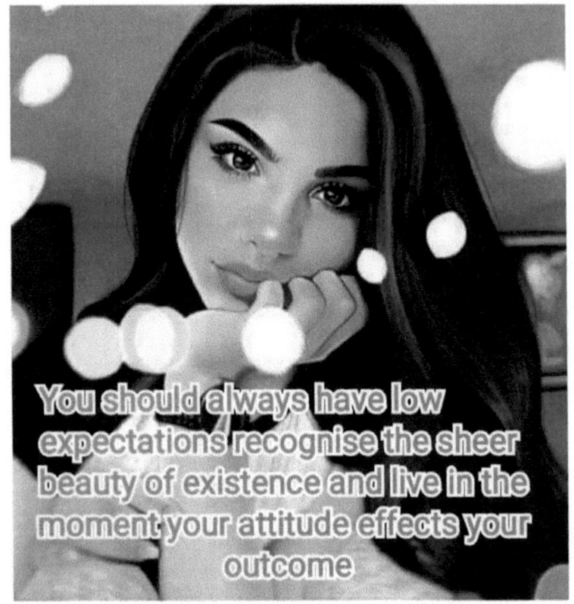

We also get defined by what we identify ourselves with.

We also are defining ourselves by what we choose to be, what we pay attention to, what we filter out.

“lit the fire within”, work on our mind

Having a creative outlet for our energy is a must..whether it is making music, painting, cooking, writing.

Rise from yours negative As you perfectly imperfect

The arrows of energy that we release always come back to our quiver.

Our intentions, thoughts, words and actions...Everything is energy.

She has infinity symbol over her crown. Shows her connection with universal energy and wisdom.

Her white dress seems to be suggest that strength comes from choosing patience, tolerance, peace and harmony..and there by gaining understaning of Universal Principles.

CHAPTER ELEVEN

ALWAYS HAPPY

More love less hate
Observation is made of purely of fact don't stuck in your own mind
Make realisation in your life
Experience the truth of actual communication and data
Word can be converted into idea
Or thought have courage to do
Anything which is the stable
Have the valuable insights
Be adjusting to the unknown
I
Inner light is the birth place of courage mind is largely responsible for the outcome in attitude
Towards a situation acknowledge
Every piece of you every experience that has formed the you that is present right now

- Be grateful: for every experience, both the good and the bad.
- Act with love: towards everyone no matter what they've done.
- Check your motives: and make sure they come from a place of love for self and others.
- Watch your attitude: because negative thoughts create angry energy directed at you.
- Forgive: It can be the hardest thing to do, but the most important in creating

CHAPTER TWELVE

UNIVERSE

@ Let your mind be stlill let it clear your thoughts design
Your framework in the path of dharma let the vision be spread into
Clear path be pure and go back to
Your vision your prayers let your power come in see with clear eyes
Have goal and determination for what comes to you let you be involved into the play ready to go there

My muses comes to me
My mind is my sanctuary
Like the golden bird of Elvis
And each begin
Hearts more believing you
Rise against the wind

Dance is about coordinated movement of body, mind, emotion, self expression.

They all need to blend together aesthetically..all focused on the song being brought to life. While dancing, there is only dance, there is no dancer (no self).

The goal of life is to make your heartbeat match the beat of the universe, to match your nature with Nature.

~Joseph Campbell,

Time to have clarity on what we choose for ourselves...

It need not be anything specific at outer reality level..but more a shift within

What kind of space feels right within

Transformation isn't sweet and bright. It's a dark and murky, painful pushing. An unravelling of the untruths you've carried in your body. A practice in facing your own created distortions. A complete uprooting before becoming" Victoria Erickson

CHAPTER THIRTEEN

DIVE IN

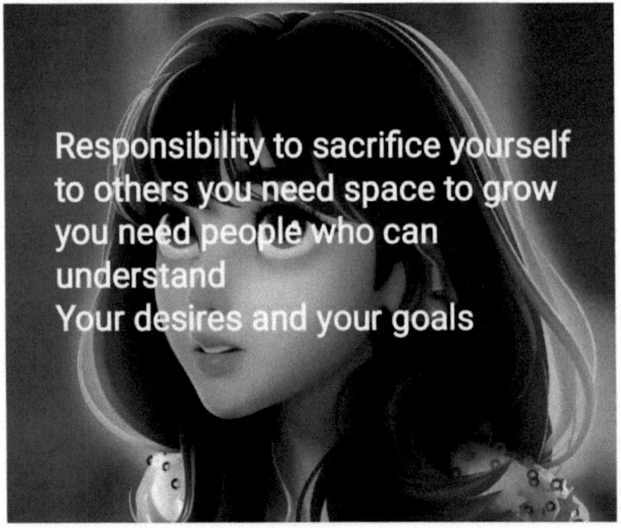

DEEP

The more you were
You need to be with yourself always
The most at your own vore being Miracles as they
They come in the form of krishna
Can be the key to
Be blessed by his
Existence follows you like a shadow
Gives you hand

I go through phases where my mind just needs to roam.

It is like just expanding without a target goal...it is exploration time.

I did go through long periods of workaholic phase.. when i focused on work, everything else faded out .

We change as we evolve. Now i balance out .

i go through intense periods of studying something...then practicing the art.. applying it .and then i need a pause...

I can see that my mind gets more brighter when work is balanced with relaxation...

CHAPTER FOURTEEN

DEEPER ACTION

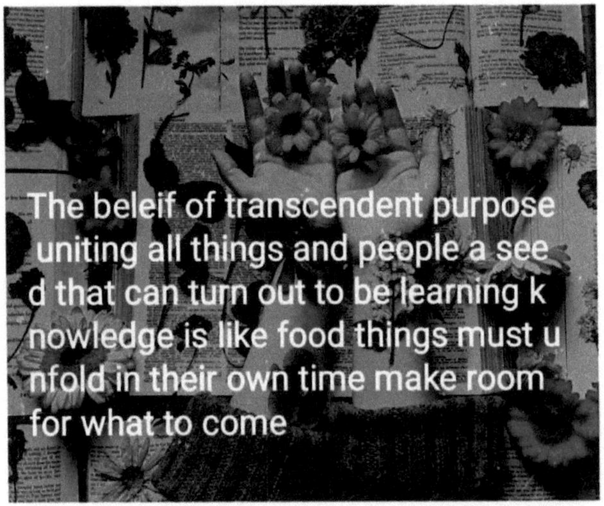

your patience is matters glow up and learn yourself

be a good listener look up for the upside and smile often everything can change the world is filled with so many beautiful souls who know the meaning of honesty The goal is to stay disciplined when everything gets tough and patient with your growth

"whats meant it will find a way"

its take a year

I was about that..here's what i saw "something old" stands for continuity;

"something new" shows optimism for the future;

"something borrowed" symbolizes borrowed happiness;

and "something blue" represents purity, love, and fidelity.

Watch yourself. Whenever you feel ambitious go and look in the mirror. You will see a certain ugliness spreading on your face, in your eyes; you will lose the grace that belongs naturally to a human being. You even lose the grace that belongs to animals. You lose the grace -- even that that belongs to rocks.

CHAPTER FIFTEEN

SEEING THROUGH

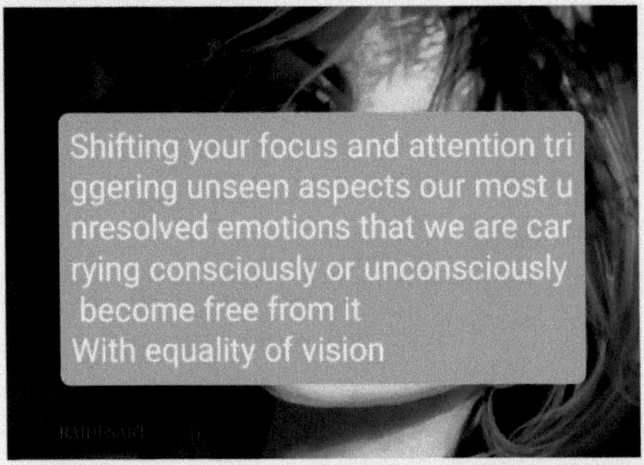

Shifting your focus and attention tri
ggering unseen aspects our most u
nresolved emotions that we are car
rying consciously or unconsciously
become free from it
With equality of vision

There's nothing to defend when life is lived as an authentic being of the earth. Then there's no justification for anger, frustration or any other emotional negativity. It's only when a part of existence becomes separate from the whole that it needs to be defended. At every level of human affairs, it's fear of being vulnerable to life with all its uncertainties that attaches the person to what is known and, subsequently, what needs to be defended.

It's said that the pure of heart is innocence personified, which is another way of saying there's nothing to defend.

It's just like a drop of water sitting on top of a flower thinking that he is a part of the flower, he falls into an animal's body and thinks that he is an animal and when it finally understands that it is water, it merges with the ocean. Then there is no discrepancy remaining between the droplet and the sea. Both were always been water but the droplet thought that it had certain identity: be it a flower or animal till all the layers covering it got destroyed.

Make a weapons out of it , make a weapons out of it...Why are you so sad, even time is waiting for your existence....

Take big leap towards the sky even sky will tremble.Incase you will fall down there will be earthquake

Know who you are know why you are hereBy starting the journey of self discovery

Even time is waiting for your existence

This search lead me to a much better understanding of not only the term, but also of my dream.

Supraconsciousness is the name Ruburt or Jane referred to for what Seth termed as the supraself, a self he explains that we are becoming in our time terms, but that we already are, and sometimes use this self in projections.

'You get what you concentrate upon. There is no other main rule.'

CHAPTER SIXTEEN

ALONE

KEY

choosing and abiding by you will be exposed to different different levels of your dependencies, weaknesses, attachments and all of this and this is what you're trying to solve. You're not trying to reach somewhere, you're getting free from your limitations

The reason we being the Absolute Un-manifest became Consciousness to manifest and to experience all this beautiful creation in every aspect of "being".

Being means existing as existence. You are the One that have taken this form to experience life this way.

Being Aware of your Awareness helps you to cognise that you being formless are experiencing life using this form so that you are not attached to the forms and suffer.

Be formless, dark, still and utterly silent and discover the true realm of simply being alive and aware and nothing else needed or desired. We are utterly alone and yet we are never lonely, singular and plural, the epitome of every paradox being exposed and clarified with no effort or thought whatsoever.

CHAPTER SEVENTEEN

BETTER VERSIONS

here is only here, now... there is no tomorrow! There is no future in which you can be happy or unhappy! You are the now, the here, Joy, Totality! Now, is not a concept of the present time in relation to the past and future, now is infinity, is Totality. Happiness has nothing to do with the circumstances, Happiness is not circumstantial! Happiness is Identity!

" Thereis no need to have any guide. If you are simple ,then simplicity is enough.

If you are natural hen know that just as the light arises from your own being meaning you are an ocean of light ... So it is that the light arises from love flowing OR NOT FLOWING FROM YOUR HEART

CHAPTER EIGHTEEN

FIGHT

suppose the tree is cut down or the tree dies & decays. What really happens then is that the atomic pile of the tree rejoins the Earth. See! The pile of atoms that extend from the Earth's surface into space is called the "tree", but once those atoms rejoin the earth upon tree decay is not called as the "tree". Rejoined atoms are now known as the "Earth." Imagine that a herb rises from the earth. What that herb contains are the earth atoms once again. But now it is a "Herb" & not the earth & The term "Earth" is no longer used now.

See! If one had a desire to a "Tree" means it was for its tree-atoms in real but that desire diminishes as it becomes the atoms of earth. When the atoms become a grass, the desire can be slightly higher than the earth. But when they go into a bull as flesh, the desire begins to increase. When they come to a person, the desire is at its maximum calling "This is me," by hugging the pile of body atoms then. Thus it will be clear to you that "desire" fluctuates upon circulation at different times for the same basic unit type.

There are so many people who want a beautiful world in which to live, where there's everlasting peace and tranquility, where there's joy and abundance. Yet these things are temporary. This is not the way of this world. It's interesting, when you stop thinking of joy, when you stop thinking of sadness,

CHAPTER NINETEEN

WILL AND WAY

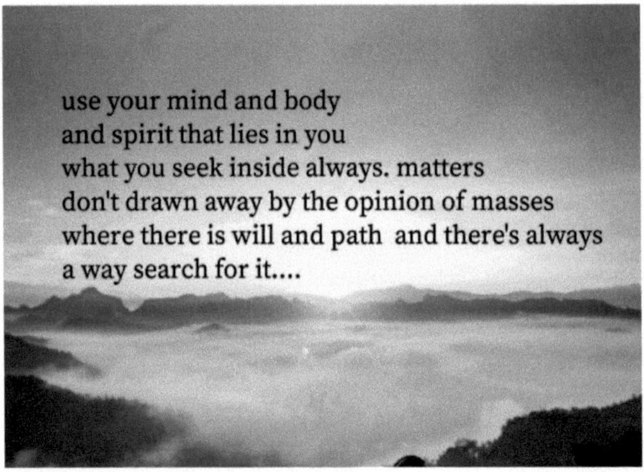

use your mind and body
and spirit that lies in you
what you seek inside always. matters
don't drawn away by the opinion of masses
where there is will and path and there's always
a way search for it....

Transform Loneliness into Stillness bestowing upon you Peace and real Fulfillment of life in every way...........Loneliness is desperation and hopelessness, stillness is fulfillment and a real Blessing. It is learning to know and Be the Reality of life. It just requires keen consistent eagerness to become the Eternal Truth of life and be resonant with the hum of its all-pervading infinite eternal Essence all the time in all walks of life.

Let each breath be an adoration for the Infinite and Eternal Energy that underlies all the forms, all the elements and all the sacrifices. It is beyond the mind to grasp its power. f there is any path? If you call the abandoning of all ideas and paths, a path, then we have a path: stillness, the zero point. Really, just knowing about it is not enough. Either you begin to abandon illusion and deal with fears that emerge from this process

You have to be a light to yourself in a world that is

utterly becoming dark " Turning this focus inward, we discover our own heart center, where true awareness naturally opens and expands infinitely. Joy and deep peacefulness settles here and we awaken to true spiritual freedom and empowerment.

The observer is real.The ego is not.This instant is in the present.

Once you judge it, you're judging the past. Be here, NOW! Forget

the previous moment. It's gone. All there is, and ever will be, is

the ever present instantaneous moment; THE HERE AND NOW

thinker . The moment you start watching the thinker , a higher level of consciousness becomes activated. You then begin to realize that there is a vast realm of intelligence beyond thought , that thought is only a tiny aspect of that intelligence. You also realize that all things that really matter – beauty , love , creativity , joy , inner peace – arise from beyond the mind. You begin to awaken. "

- Working on non-judgment
- Working on acceptance
- Working on forgiveness
- Working on not concluding
- Working on self-improvement
- Working on development Awareness

#shiftingintoawareness #newearth #fifthdimension #TheGreatReset

CHAPTER TWENTY

PLAY SMART

We should not run away from complications, we should not run away from challenges, but we should face them with a simple heart. A heart of devotion. A heart of integrity and character. A heart of seva, love and devotion.

Sometimes it seems that life is full of obstacles and miseries.
But it is only because we do not have the goal clear in our heart.
Sometimes we deal with too much stress and worry,
but it's because we do not know the peace within ourselves.
Sometimes we feel it's all the other people who get lucky,
But it's because we have not tapped our own luck fulfilling faith.

The basic idea,is to have an informal chat with you on the specific subject of your spiritual journey even while living . You may want a little help in understanding an experience or sometimes you may want to talk about what problem is distracting you from your goals;

GOOD VIBES ONLY

9 798886 671216

Printed by Libri Plureos GmbH in Hamburg, Germany